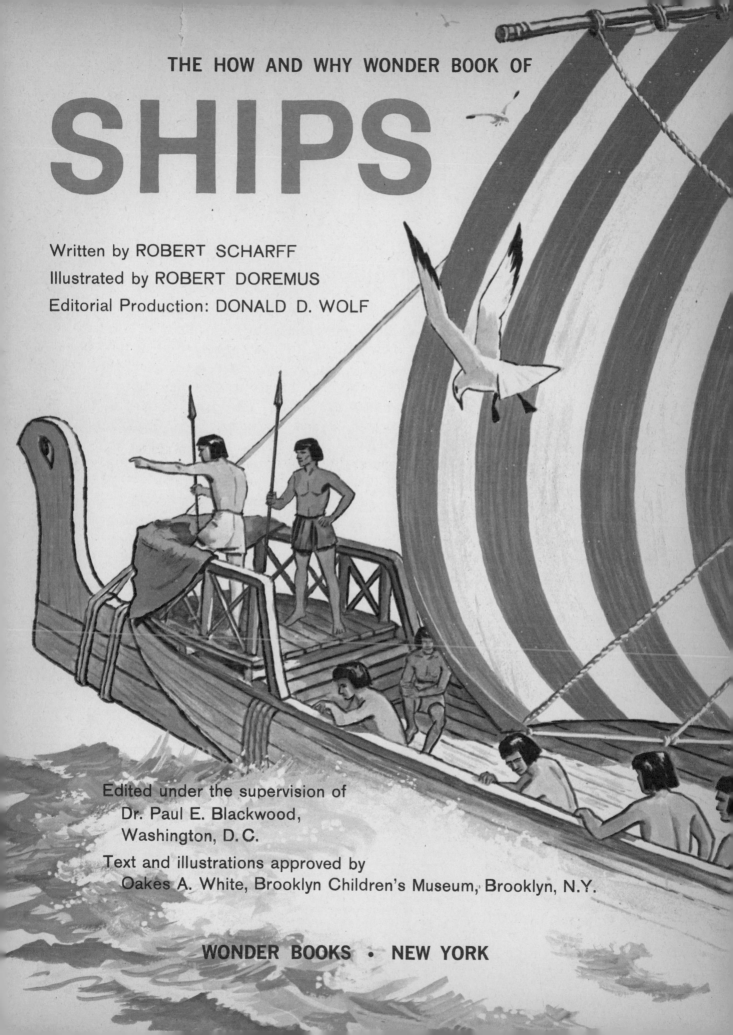

THE HOW AND WHY WONDER BOOK OF

SHIPS

Written by ROBERT SCHARFF

Illustrated by ROBERT DOREMUS

Editorial Production: DONALD D. WOLF

Edited under the supervision of
Dr. Paul E. Blackwood,
Washington, D.C.

Text and illustrations approved by
Oakes A. White, Brooklyn Children's Museum, Brooklyn, N.Y.

WONDER BOOKS • NEW YORK

Introduction

Picture a floating tree; perhaps this was the first boat. Picture a nuclear-powered submarine encircling the world without surfacing. Between these two kinds of water craft, literally hundreds of different types of boats have been developed through the centuries. But we must be careful not to say *boat* when we mean *ship*. Such a mistake will mark us as a "landlubber," a shore person, one among millions everywhere. To many people, the differences between a sloop, a cutter, a yawl, a schooner, or a ketch are not clear. This *How and Why Wonder Book of Ships* comes to the rescue of everyone as it clarifies the history, lore, uses, and kinds of ships from the earliest times to the present.

There are various ways to study ships. What makes them go? Muscle power, wind, steam, electricity, nuclear energy? What are their uses? Commerce, fishing, travel, war, pleasure? What kinds of ships are there? Freighters, cruisers, yachts, whaling factories? What crews are needed? Sailors, captains, stewards and engineers? Whatever the approach, we shall see that the use and control of the sea has always been important to the growth and economic well being of nations. We shall see that the variety of kinds and uses of ships is almost beyond belief.

In social studies classes, this *How and Why Wonder Book of Ships* will aid pupils in their study of exploration and will show how ships are related to the fortunes of nations in war and peace. In science classes, it will be useful in the study of floating objects and power. It will stimulate all readers to think not only about ships of the past and present, but also about those of the future.

Paul E. Blackwood

Dr. Blackwood is a professional employee in the U. S. Office of Education. This book was edited by him in his private capacity and no official support or endorsement by the Office of Education is intended or should be inferred.

Contents

PRIMITIVE MAN ASTRIDE
SINGLE LOG

EARLY RAFT

DUGOUT WITH PADDLE

ANIMAL SKIN
USED AS SAIL

ESKIMO KAYAK

INDIAN BIRCHBARK CANOE

EARLY EGYPTIAN SHIP ON STONE RELIEF

RECONSTRUCTION OF
EGYPTIAN TRADING SHIP
ABOUT 1500 B.C.

EGYPTIAN
REED RIVERBOAT
ABOUT 2000 B.C.

GREEK VASE WITH PAINTING
OF EARLY TRADING SHIP

PHOENICIAN BIREME

WARSHIP

GREEK BIREME ABOUT 500 B.C.

The First Ships

Who invented the first boat? No one knows exactly how or when man first had the idea to travel by ship. Perhaps thousands of years ago, primitive men watched a tree trunk, with a small animal resting on it, float down a river. The men wondered if a fallen tree would bear a man in the water. Once they tried, they found it would. In time, man discovered he did not need the whole trunk; a log would do just as well. While sitting astride his log boat, he found that he could propel himself by paddling with his hands and feet.

That single log was then succeeded by several logs bound together by pieces of hide or bark. This raft could float the owner, his family and his household goods. One of these early sailors found that instead of churning the water with his hands and feet, he could use a pole to push against the bank or bottom of the stream. Still later, the pole was shaped into a paddle, and voyages were made farther out from shore, into deeper water. As time passed, better rafts were made. The sides were built up and a platform on deck protected the traveler's cargo from the waves.

Then, someone must have hollowed out a log with fire or with his crude stone tools. Although clumsy, awkward, and heavy, these dug-out logs could float and carry considerable weight. They also had a certain advantage over the raft because they could be handled more easily by a single paddler.

Next came a master-builder who covered a light frame of wood with long strips of bark or the skins of animals. This was a great step forward. Here was a light craft that could be propelled with ease, yet was strong enough to carry several passengers.

With the step from the primitive raft to the frame boat with sides and a keel came an advance in the method of propulsion. One day, somebody must have noticed that as he stood or sat upon his raft, the wind seemed to help carry him along. Eagerly he hung an animal skin from a slender pole, stuck it into his boat, and was rewarded by moving faster than ever before. Thus the sail was discovered. And he found that, just as the paddle pushed him through the water, so would it steer his crude vessel.

There are still primitive craft in use today — the African log canoe, the woven basket boat of India, the south sea island outrigger, and Eskimo kayak. Each year many of us use canoes — a direct descendant of the American Indian's birch canoe — to paddle up rivers and across lakes.

Who built the first real ships? As civilization progressed, boats became necessary for trade, travel and warfare. The demand increased for a ship with speed, size and equipment to cruise, to carry cargo, to defend itself and to attack an enemy. Since the cradle of modern civilization was in the lands around the Mediterranean Sea, it is believed that ships bearing an actual resemblance to those of today came from this region. Archaeologists have found clear pictures of sailing ships and even a few model ships with sails in the tombs of Egyptian Kings. These models were placed in the tombs so that the spirits of the dead could be transported to the land of their afterlife. These model ships are probably good copies of ships then in use and give us a good idea what the early Egyptian ships were like.

More than three thousand years before the Christian era, the Egyptians were carrying on commerce in corn and cattle along the Nile River and over the Red Sea. They used flimsy boats made of reeds tied together because not much wood was available in Egypt.

Egyptians also tied a rope from the bow to the stern to keep the curved ends of the ship from drooping into the water. A single-pole mast was punched right through the bottom of the boat and the hole around the pole made watertight. From this mast, they hung a sail. These boats would sail ahead of the wind and a little to either side, but as soon as the wind was crosswise, the sail was lowered and the paddlers had to work to move the ship.

By about 1500 B. C., the Egyptians made their merchant ships much more seaworthy by building them of wooden planks imported from Phoenicia, on the eastern shore of the Mediterranean. The design of reed boats with high bow (front) and stern (back) was now built of wood. Thus the hull was improved and the sail could be raised and lowered. Steering was done by using paddles, sometimes four or five, but more generally one or two bound together and fastened to an upright post. Thus the paddle could be worked like a tiller or rudder.

Egyptian warships of this period were similar to their merchant ships except that they had bulwarks (extended sides) to protect the rowers and amidships there was a raised deck to enable the soldiers to use their bows and arrows and hurl their spears over the heads of the oarsmen. Sometimes at the top of the mast, there was a bell-shaped platform where an expert archer or slinger was stationed, somewhat like the sharpshooters in the maintop of later ships.

The history of Egypt after 1200 B. C. was marked mostly by decline. Large areas of land were lost and mastery of the seas was gradually taken over by the Phoenicians. The Egyptians were not mainly a seafaring people by nature, and the ships they constructed and equipped for sea-going voyages were actually specially reinforced rivercraft developed for use on the Nile. They were wonderful builders and engineers, but their natural home was the river and not the sea. The Phoenicians, on the other hand, were sea-roving people who dared to

Who were the ancient sailors of the Mediterranean Sea?

SEATING OF OARSMEN IN BIREME

SEATING OF OARSMEN IN TRIREME

ROMAN TRADING VESSEL

ROMAN WAR GALLEY 200 B.C.

leave the Mediterranean, traveled along the coasts of Spain and France and England and even circumnavigated the African continent. These people dominated Mediterranean trade from around 1200 B. C. until about 1 A. D.

Unfortunately, we know very little about the design of Phoenician ships, and the little we do know comes from Egyptian and Greek portrayals. From these drawings, it is believed that Phoenicians invented the *bireme galley,* a vessel with two rows of oars, one above the other, and also the *trireme galley,* which had three banks of oars similarly arranged. With this additional oar power, they gained more speed without increasing the length of their ship. Thus, the Phoenicians were able to make much longer voyages than earlier seafarers.

The Greeks, through their mythology and the writings of their poet Homer, have left us heroic pictures of the years that Greece

What was ancient Greece's contribution to ship design?

was a seapower — 1200 B. C. to 300 B.C. The early Greeks used ships that were copied from the Phoenicians with whom they traded. The early Greek biremes carried crews of 50 to 120 men, all of whom, except the commander, took turns at the oars.

There was a great difference between the merchant ships and those intended for warfare. The merchantmen were broad and slow-moving, built to carry large cargoes. The warships were narrow and swift, constructed for speed in the chase. The trireme was the warship of Athens during the Golden Age of Greece, though many of her galleys carried more than three rows of oars. Some had four and some five banks of rowers. The men of the lowest bench used the shortest oars. The rowers sat in tiers, one man to an oar, and the benches extended from the inner side

of the hull to timbers built between the decks. Some triremes had one mast, some two, each with a single sail, and the sails as well as the hulls were painted bright colors. Hulls were extremely ornate, often ending in a carved figure or animal head. The war galleys had a castle-like structure built on their decks, from which missiles could be thrown at the enemy; this was the origin of the word *forecastle*. Many of these galleys carried a dangerous, metal-sheathed ram at the water's edge, below the figurehead, for the purpose of ramming enemy vessels in battle.

As civilization moved westward along the Mediterranean and Greek power began to decline after 300 B. C., Rome and Carthage — the powerful

Who succeeded Greece as the chief sea power?

colony established by the Phoenicians in the North African region now called Tunisia — took up the battle for world supremacy. While the Romans had a great army, they had no navy to match the great fleet of Carthage. But the Romans had to have ships to combat Carthage and they knew very little about building them. Then one day, around 260 B. C., fortune wrecked a Carthaginian quinquireme — a five-banked ship — on the Italian shore. The Romans hauled the quinquireme out, studied her, measured her, and so learned how to construct a galley. Crews were taught to row in a framework of benches set up on dry land. The Romans built and launched a fleet in the 60 days after the felling of the first timber.

This first Roman fleet was badly beaten by the more experienced sailors of Carthage off the Italian coast; then the Romans built a more powerful fleet. In the new fleet, the inventive Romans constructed what was called a *corvus*, a bridge that could be dropped onto an enemy vessel and that would hold its

place by a heavy iron hook that fastened into the deck. By this bridge, Roman soldiers could board the enemy ship and fight the enemy hand-to-hand, a form of combat in which they had long been successful on shore. By this means, the new fleet defeated Carthage at Mylae in 260 B. C. and eventually won the command of the Mediterranean Sea.

The oarsmen of the war galleys were rarely Romans; they were usually conquered foreigners, prisoners, or slaves. The frequent Roman wars provided the victors with plenty of captives to pull the sweeps. The Romans became such successful shipbuilders that, when Caesar prepared to invade Britain in 55 B. C., he set up a shipyard at Boulogne on the French coast. There 600 vessels to carry his army and supplies were built in a very short time.

To carry on trade with their widespread empire, the Romans also built merchant ships. The merchantmen were quite different from the warships because sails, not oars, were the primary means of propulsion. If a merchant ship were to carry enough cargo to make money, it could not carry many slave rowers or food for them. These ships carried a great more sail area for their size than did the war galleys. The Roman warships had only one mast; many merchant vessels carried three masts, each with a sail, and sometimes one of the masts had a square topsail as well. Ships with several masts used no oars; they were propelled by sails alone.

About 8 A. D., a different and a much sturdier type of ship was developed in the Baltic Sea area off the Scandinavian peninsula. This was the double-ended ship of the

Who were the first sailors to cross the Atlantic Ocean?

Norsemen which usually is referred to as the *Viking longship* or *drakkar*. These ships, low and long with curving bow (front) and stern (back), were built to weather the roughest seas. The most popular type was about 80 feet in length, built of oak wood throughout. It had places for 32 oars, 16 on a side, and along the gunwales (the sides) were hung a row of wooden shields to protect the oarsmen against wind and water spray. The longship carried a single sail much wider at the foot than at the top and it was decorated in brilliant colors or embroidered in gold. The figurehead at the bow was that of a fierce dragon which the Vikings believed would scare their enemies, or sea serpents which they thought roamed the ocean. The dragon head was detachable and it was forbidden by Viking law to carry it when a ship neared the shores of home because it would scare their own people. At night, the crew spread a tent over the deck and slept in leather bags. Since they could not cook at sea, they ate dried meat, dried bread, nuts, and meal mixed with fat.

They washed the food down with water or strong liquor. The same type of ship was used for both commerce and warfare. Small boats very similar to the drakkers are still in use in Scandinavian countries and in Scotland.

The Norsemen were fearless and hardy sailors. They made many raids on Britain, and even sailed into the Mediterranean. One Norseman, Leif Ericson, while on his way to make a raid on Greenland in about 1000 A. D., was blown off course by easterly winds and carried across the Atlantic to what is now Labrador. He stayed there for a whole winter to repair his ship and to gather food before making the trip back across the Atlantic. Other Norsemen, in their quest for adventure and wealth, may have even sailed as far as the land that is now the United States.

The recorded history of ships begins on the Nile, the Aegean Sea around Greece and the Mediterranean. But from the Norsemen came the first great race of sea rovers, the direct forefathers of the English merchant adventurers and the Yankee clipper ship captains.

The Age of Sailing

Very little advancement in the design of ships was made during the Middle Ages, which lasted from about 500 A. D. to about 1500

What made the age of exploration possible?

A. D. The need for exploration, for new horizons, trade and conquest did not seem to exist and man's economic interests were limited to the land. To some extent, small ships were developed to maintain the island trade and to ply

Above, the *Santa Maria, Nina* and *Pinta*. The *Santa Maria*, Columbus' flagship on his voyage in 1492 to the New World, was a typical 15th century caravel. The *Mayflower*, right, which brought the Pilgrims to America in 1620, was a bark. A bark is a vessel with three or more masts, all square-rigged except the for-and-aft-rigged aftermast.

the paths of the inland seas. But the large ship for ocean voyages was almost unknown after the fall of the Roman Empire until the 14th century.

During this century, Italian, Spanish and Portuguese shipbuilders started redesigning the Roman merchantman to make it more seaworthy and to make it powered only by sails. Their work resulted in a new type of sailing ship called the *caravel*.

The caravel, which varied slightly with each shipbuilder, was high-sided, broad and deep. She had a square stern with a rudder in the center of the stern. But she still had the curved bow and flat bottom similar to the galley and viking ships. The caravel had a high structure at the bow called the *forecastle*, and a still higher structure of two

decks at the stern called the *stern castle*. These castles were used for living quarters and also kept great waves from sweeping over the decks. Some of the first caravels had a single mainmast, and it was not long before a second one called a *mizzenmast* was placed behind the mainmast. Soon, a third mast, the *foremast*, was added in front of the mainmast to give more power to the ship. Both the foremast and mainmasts carried square sails, while the mizzenmast held a triangular sail, called a *lateen* sail. The three-corner lateen sail was placed in a fore-and-aft (front-to-back) position, while the square sails were always placed athwartships (across the ship or at right angles to the fore-and-aft sail). The square sails gave the ship great power and speed with a favorable wind. The lateen sail helped with the maneuvers such as going against the wind (tacking) and steering the ship. Some of the later 16th century caravels had a fourth mast added, which carried a lateen sail, while others were designed with various other sail arrangements to make them handle more easily and travel faster.

A caravel was the type of ship used by Christopher Columbus on his first voyage across the Atlantic in 1492, and by Spanish and Portuguese sailors of the 1500's and 1600's. Ships of this design were used for exploration, long voyages, and commerce.

The *galleon* was a bigger, more advanced type of caravel,

What is a galleon? and had a round bottom instead of the flat style used earlier. (Sixteenth century caravels also used a round bottom since it made the ship more seaworthy.) The galleon was at first an Italian armed

merchant vessel. About 1550, King Henry VIII of England developed this craft into a great ship. The early galleon had both heavy fore and mainmasts which carried deep square sails, and one or two small masts toward the rear which held lateen sails. A long, raised deck, called the *quarterdeck*, ran from the mainmast toward the rear of the ship, where a still higher deck, called the *poop,* was located. The forecastle, or raised deck in front of the foremast, was square and rather low. The sides of galleon warships were usually pierced for mounting guns or cannons. Sometimes there were guns above deck.

The galleon was widely used by the maritime powers — England, Spain, France, and Holland — in the 16th century for both commerce and war. During the 17th century, shipbuilders increased the number and area of the sails and made the hull still more seaworthy. Galleons were used until the early part of the 19th century.

A ship of the Spanish Armada (above).

A three-decker English galleon of the late 16th century, the time of Queen Elizabeth.

13

THE U.S. FRIGATE CONSTITUTION

THE YANKEE CLIPPER LIGHTNING (1854)

During the 17th century, shipbuilders began to develop a new type of ship called a war frigate. The term *frigate* gradually came to mean a warship whose guns were set up on a single whole deck, a quarterdeck, and a forecastle. The frigate became famous in American history during the War of 1812 between the United States and Great Britain. Best known, of course, is the *Constitution,* or *Old Ironsides* as she was proudly called by her crew, since they claimed that enemy cannon balls bounced off her hard wooden planks. This war was chiefly a frigate's war, and the American frigates were found to be much more heavily armed and much faster than the English frigates as the British discovered to their distress on several occasions.

What is a frigate?

After the War of 1812, frigates were used until the introduction of the steamship. As a matter of fact, many of the first steamships were frigates converted from sail power to steam power.

The peak of perfection in the sailing ship was reached by the American or Yankee clipper. The clipper ship had high masts and many large sails. Her overhanging bow curved in and back from a sharp point forward. She appeared in the 1840's and was used principally on the long voyages to the West Coast, India, and China, often sailing as fast and 24 knots an hour with favoring winds, faster than many cargo ships today. But clipper ships were doomed by the coming of the steamship. A few small clippers were built after 1862. But for all practical purposes, almost five thousand years of sailing ships ended about 1900.

What was the most perfect sailing vessel?

While sailing vessels are no longer used for commercial or military purposes, they are still favored pleasure craft. Pleasure sailing vessels are classified accord-

What kind of sailboats are used today?

GAFF SLOOP

MARCONI SLOOP

CATBOAT

SQUARE-TOPSAIL SLOOP

CUTTER

ing to their *rig* or sail plan. Let us take a look at the various rigs in the order of simplicity.

Catboat. Has a single mast, forward in the boat, and carries a single triangular fore-and-aft sail called the *mainsail*. This type rig is the simplest and the easiest with which to learn to sail.

Sloop. Has a single mast and, in addition to the mainsail, carries a smaller triangular fore-and-aft sail, called a *jibsail*, forward of the mast. The sloop is better controlled than the catboat because the sail area is broken up into two sails, making the handling of a larger boat easier.

Cutter. Has one mast, but two jibs. The inner jib is called a *staysail* and is carried under the jibsail. This extra sail makes the cutter sail faster than a sloop.

Yawl. In recent years, the yawl rig has found high favor with ocean-racing yachtsmen. This is a handy rig with the sails divided on two masts. The shorter of the two masts is called the *mizzenmast* and is placed behind the mainmast. The same sails carried on the sloop and the cutter may be carried, plus a hard-pulling *mizzen staysail*.

Ketch. Similar to the yawl, except that the mizzenmast is longer and mizzen staysail is larger. This type of rig is a favorite among deep-sea voyagers when speed is desired.

Schooner. This rig is seldom used by yachtsmen, but is a favorite of commercial fishermen in many parts of the world. Almost all schooners are two-masted and the back or aftermast is al-

ways the taller. The most common rig carries two jibsails: a gaff foresail with a small "fisherman's staysail" over it, and the mainsail. A great variety of other sails can be used in a schooner rig.

Sailing for pleasure and for competition has never lost its thrill for thousands of watersports fans throughout the world. One of the most demanding competitions is the race for the America's Cup. The possession of the Cup, a trophy in international yachting, is the symbol of the world's sailboat racing supremacy. It is named the America's Cup for a yacht named *America* that won a big race held by England in 1851. The *America*, and every yacht that has held this cup since, has been from the United States. Most challengers for the cup have been British except one Canadian and, in 1962, an unsuccessful Australian attempt to break the U.S. streak of success.

What is the most coveted sailing trophy?

America's cup 1962: The American yacht, Weatherly, defeats the Australian challenger, Gretel.

YAWL   KETCH   SCHOONER

JOUFFROY'S STEAMBOAT

STEVEN'S SS PHOENIX

FULTON'S CLERMONT

FITCH'S STEAMBOAT

The Age of Steam

Who invented the steamship?

In the closing decades of the 18th century many experiments were made with steam propulsion of boats. Contrary to many school history books, Robert Fulton, an American inventor, did *not* build the first steamship. No one invented the steamship, but Fulton did build a practical one that started their general use.

In the mid-1700's, James Watt, a Scotsman, made improvements on the steam engine that made it possible to run ships with this new source of power. While many people tried, it was not until 1783 that a Frenchman, Claude de Jouffroy, built the first successful steamboat. Because of the political unrest which preceded the French Revolution, de Jouffroy's shipbuilding was not given official support and was abandoned.

In 1787, John Fitch built the first American steamship. While this craft was not too successful, she did operate regularly for a short time on the Delaware River between Philadelphia and Trenton, New Jersey.

The first steamship to engage in commercially successful operations was Robert Fulton's famous wooden-hulled paddle-wheeler, the *SS Clermont,* which steamed up the Hudson River on August 17, 1807. The *SS Clermont* carried scheduled passenger service between Albany and New York City.

The year that Fulton built his ship, Colonel John Stevens constructed the paddle steamer *SS Phoenix* at New York. Many people of that time thought the *SS Phoenix* was a better ship, but she was completed a little too late. Fulton not only received all the glory, but the sole right to operate steamships on all New York State waterways. Two years later, Stevens took his ship to Philadelphia, where she was operated for several years.

The trip from Hoboken, New Jersey — near New York — to Philadelphia made the *SS Phoenix* the first steamboat to go to sea. (The letters *SS* are generally used to distinguish a ship powered by steam.)

16

SS SAVANNAH DRIVEN BY
A SIDE PADDLE-WHEEL

The first ship to use steam in an Atlantic crossing was the *SS Savannah*, also a wooden-hulled paddle-wheeler.

What was the first steamship to cross the Atlantic?

The ship left Savannah, Georgia, on May 22, 1819, and arrived at Liverpool, England, on June 20. She was built as a sailing ship, and her engine was used about 105 hours in the 30-day trip. Because the *SS Savannah* used her sails for most of her journey, she cannot truthfully be called the first steamship to make a transatlantic voyage. When the ship returned to the United States, the owners took the engine out and she became a sailing ship again.

Various other sailing ships were fitted out with steam engines and paddle-wheels, but not until 1838 did a vessel cross the Atlantic Ocean entirely under steam power. In that year, two British companies decided to compete in North Atlantic travel, and their rival ships left Britain within a few days of each other in a race for New York. The *SS Sirius* was the first to arrive in New York Harbor. Six hours later the *SS Great West-*ern came up the Narrows in New York harbor, throwing off great clouds of black smoke while shore cannons saluted, church bells tolled, and thousands of people shouted and waved. With the arrival of these two English ships in America, the age of steam began.

Most of the earlier steamships used paddle-wheels to move them through the water. The side-wheelers had a big paddle-wheel on each side partly under water, so that when the paddles were moving they were pushing on water. (We can see a resemblance to the wheels of an automobile, which while turning forward push backward on the ground and thus make the vehicle go forward.) Thus, while the paddle-wheels are pushing a stream of water back on each side of the ship, the reaction to that push makes the ship move ahead.

How were the early steamships propelled?

In the late 1700's and early 1800's inventors in the United States, England, and France began experimenting with

JACOB STRADER

screw propellers for ships. John Fitch and Colonel John Stevens of steamboat building fame worked with propellers shaped like wood screws. But it was John Ericsson, a Swedish-American, who developed the first successful bladed propeller similar to those used today. In 1845, the *SS Great Britain* became the first propeller-driven ship to cross the North Atlantic. While the screw-propelled steamship was beyond doubt more efficient than the paddle-wheeler, the traveling public did not immediately accept the new development in steamships. To them the paddle-wheel offered visible reassurance of a

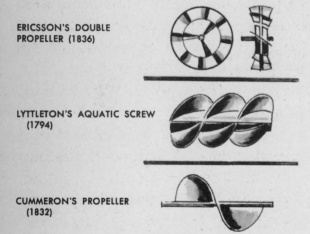

ERICSSON'S DOUBLE
PROPELLER (1836)

LYTTLETON'S AQUATIC SCREW
(1794)

CUMMERON'S PROPELLER
(1832)

ship's power. But by 1855, the paddle-wheel was replaced by propellers on most steamships.

As we know, an engine is a machine that

How does a steam engine make a ship go?

changes energy into some form of useful mechanical work. A ship's engine burns or consumes fuel in order to heat water to produce steam. The heat energy contained by the steam is released by various mechanical methods to cause a shaft to rotate. As the

shaft turns, the propeller connected to it at the stern of the ship also rotates. The propeller has from three to five curved blades that suck the water in ahead of them and force it out behind them. The pressure of this powerful backward stream of water as it presses against the surrounding water pushes the ship forward. While most small ships have but one propeller, the larger ones have at least two, and some have as many as four. The additional propellers help to increase the ship's power and make the vessel easier to handle.

The first steam engines used were rather

What type of steam engines are used aboard ships?

simple. The paddle-wheel or propeller was driven directly from the engine. In 1854, the compound engine was introduced. In these *reciprocating steam engines* (similar to those used on railroad locomotives), the steam pushed a double piston that

turned a crankshaft attached to the propeller shaft of the ship. In this arrangement, more power was developed from the same amount of steam. But, the reciprocating steam engine, by modern standards, is inefficient and slow, and today's ships seldom use it.

The steam turbine engine developed by an Englishman, Charles A. Parsons, in 1884 is still in use today. In this engine, the steam from a boiler spins a turbine that drives the propeller. Most of the recently-constructed steamships use a turbo-electric drive system. In this, the steam turbine does not drive the propeller directly; it drives a generator that supplies electricity for a motor. The electric motor then turns the propeller.

The story of the fuel that has driven vessels over the seas is one of the most interesting parts of the history of steamships. The coal bunkers (bins) necessary for the earliest steamships took up so much space that those ships found their cargo-carrying capacity very limited. When the *SS Sirius* made her voyage in 1838, she sailed from Cork, Ireland, with 95 passengers and 450 tons of coal. She arrived in New York 18 days later, but to do so, she had scraped the coalbins and supplemented her coal with the ship's fittings and furniture. To save on coal, steamships carried auxiliary sails until the 1880's.

What fuels are used to drive steam engines?

During World War I, the conversion of the world's merchant fleet from coal to petroleum began. Most ships were coal-burners in that day, partly because the British owned about half of the world's merchant fleet and were then the world's principal supplier of coal. When the United States, which had an adequate supply of petroleum, built a large fleet during World War I, the ships were oil-burners. In 1914, coal accounted for 90 per cent of ships' fuel. Shortly after World War II it accounted for approximately 25 per cent.

Petroleum has many advantages over coal for marine fuel because oil "packs a much greater punch" than coal, and oil saves storage space. Moreover, oil can be stored between the double bottoms of modern ships or in tanks located in places on the ship not suitable for cargo. Oil is cleaner, and the loading process takes only a few hours instead of the three or four days required for coal.

With the completion of the first nuclear-powered merchant vessel *NS Savannah* (named in honor of the original

SS Savannah of 1819), we have started a new age of ships. (The letters *NS* stand for nuclear ship.) On these atomic-powered ships, the heat that turns the water into steam comes from a nuclear reactor rather than from an oil furnace. In other words, the nuclear reactor does not drive the ship's propellers as many believe, but just replaces oil as a source of fuel. Just as oil offered advantages over coal, so does atomic power over oil. An average oil-burning ship can travel three times as far without refueling as one using coal as a fuel. On the other hand, the atomic submarine *Nautilus* (see page 42) cruised since 1954 refueling only three times, and an atomic powered surface ship might equal that record.

While steam engines and steam turbines are used for big ships, a **What is a motor ship?** number of smaller craft use gasoline engines (similar to automobile motors) and larger ones have diesel engines. A ship that is driven by either a gasoline or diesel engine is called a *motor ship*.

A motor ship equipped with a diesel engine burns heavy oil directly in its cylinders, just as a car motor burns gasoline, and thus requires no boiler or furnace as does a steamship. The space saved by having no boilers can be used for storage of cargo. Also, a motor ship is more economical on fuel and needs no lengthy "warming up" as a steam engine does. (Before a steamship can get underway, the boilers must be "fired up" until the water boils so that steam is present to drive her, and this sometimes takes as long as 24 hours.) However, most diesel-driven ships are slower than steamships and can be used only in smaller passenger and cargo ships, ferries, and tug boats, fireboats, yachts, and smaller military vessels.

Modern motor ships have either geared-drive or diesel-electric machinery. On a geared-drive ship, the diesel

The first battle between ironclad ships, the Civil War encounter of the Union *Monitor* and the Confederate *Merrimac* on March 8, 1862, told the world that wooden fighting ships belonged to the past.

MERRIMAC

MONITOR

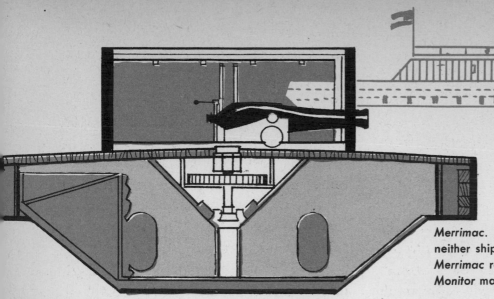

Cross section through the *Monitor* (left), her hull almost entirely below the waterline. She was designed by the Swedish engineer, John Ericsson.

Above, a schematic sideview of the *Merrimac*. The battle was indecisive because neither ship destroyed the other. But since the *Merrimac* retreated after hours of fighting, the *Monitor* may be considered the victor.

engine works through a series of gears to turn the propeller. On a diesel-electric ship, the engine turns a generator which supplies electricity to operate a motor that is connected to the propelling apparatus.

During the time of conversion from sail to steam, an equally important revolution in construction was under way. The early steamships were built of wood, but experiments in the use of iron for the hulls of ships had been made even before the end of the 18th century. Most shipbuilders had been afraid to use iron because they feared that iron, being heavier than water, would impair the ship's floating capacity. The British ship *Vulcan,* built in 1818, was the first all-iron sailing vessel. But not until between 1845 and 1880 did iron come more into general use, gradually replacing wood for large steamships. In 1881, the British *SS Servia,* became one of the first all-steel ships to cross the Atlantic. All modern ships are of steel construction.

When were steel ships introduced?

The Greek mathematician Archimedes discovered the principle that explains why a ship floats. He found that any object placed in a liquid is buoyed upward by a force equal to the weight of the liquid displaced by the object. Thus, an object floats when its weight is less than the weight of an equal volume of water. An object sinks when its weight is greater than the weight of an equal volume of water. If one cubic foot of steel weighing 500 pounds is placed in water, it will displace a cubic foot of water weighing 62.5 pounds. Since its weight is eight times heavier than the cubic foot of water, the block of steel sinks rapidly.

Why does a steel ship float?

But steel ships can float. How? If you cut the cubic foot of steel into thin sheets, you could fasten the sheets together to make a box about six feet long, six feet wide, and five feet high. Your box contains 6 x 6 x 5 feet or 180 cubic feet. Will it sink? Remember that 180 cubic feet of the steel box still weigh 500 pounds. On the other hand, 180 cubic feet of displaced water weigh 180 x 62.5 or 11,250 pounds, more than 22 times the weight of the steel box. So the steel box, weighing 500 pounds, is more than 22 times lighter than 180 cubic feet of water weighing 11,250 pounds. Thus the steel box floats.

How is the speed of a ship measured? The *knot* is the measure of a ship's speed and is given in the number of *nautical* miles covered in an hour. A nautical mile is 6,080 feet; a land mile is 5,280 feet. The speed of a ship, when given in knots per hour, cannot be compared with the speed of an automobile in miles per hour, because a nautical mile is about 800 feet longer than a mile on shore. Therefore a ship making 35 knots will be going as fast as a car going almost 40 miles per hour.

What is the tradition of the sea? The tradition of the sea is the specific customs and language of the men who sail the ships. You will note that we said "sail" the ships. While sailing ships are seldom used today, it is still the tradition of sailors to say that a ship "sails," even though she has no sails aboard. It is also traditional to use the letter "a" as a prefix for "on" or "in," as in *amidships* — meaning on or in the middle of a ship, *aboard* — on or in a vessel, *astern* — meaning on or in the back.

A sailor also always refers to a ship as *she*. While no one knows why, one theory is that the Greeks gave their ships female names to honor Athena, the goddess of warships. Also anyone who calls a ship a boat is immediately labeled a *landlubber* — a shore person. *Boat* is a term used only for small craft, usually propelled by oars, outboard motors and small sails. Among the boats in the merchant marine and the navy are the life-boats carried on a ship's deck and the PT boats.

The tradition of the sea has some noble customs. For example, it is traditional for all ships to come to the aid of one in trouble. When an SOS (the international distress signal) is sent out over a ship's radio, all vessels nearby immediately change their course, or direction, and come to the aid of the ship in distress. When rescue is necessary, it is the motto of the seas that women and children are the first to be saved. Also it is traditional for the captain of a sinking ship to be the last person alive to leave her.

One of the first American packets to use steam in transatlantic crossings was the SS *Arctic*. She was struck in heavy fog by a French vessel off the coast of Newfoundland and sank.

The U. S. Merchant Marine

The merchant marine can be defined as "the commercial ships of a nation, privately or publicly owned, as distinct from the navy.

How did the merchant marine help build America?

From the beginning, commercial or merchant ships have played an important part in the history of the United States. From a few scattered groups of isolated colonists in a strange land, merchant ships have helped a country to become a rich and powerful leader among nations of the world.

The American colonists became skillful sailors and shipbuilders and shrewd traders. Their ships sailed over all the oceans and appeared in every port, and their country grew and prospered. They invented new types of ships, the schooner and the clipper, faster and more beautiful than any sailing ship known before. They sold ships to other countries, earning much needed foreign exchange. By the end of the 18th century, American ships carried most of the country's growing trade.

Shipping was not without its dangers

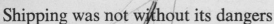

and difficulties. Coasts were uncharted and navigation aids few. Quarters on shipboard were cramped, food was monotonous and often bad. Every war meant the loss of many vessels from enemy attack. The United States had lost the protection of the British fleet after the Revolution and had no real navy of its own until after 1800. American ships were often under attack by pirates or were subject to restrictions by other powers such as France and Spain.

After the War of 1812 with Great Britain, when the United States objected to the seizing of her merchant seamen for service in the British navy, American shipping enjoyed 40 years of expansion. This expansion was accompanied by many improvements in shipbuilding and navigation.

The earliest American ships sailed whenever cargo was offered. Often the captain and crew undertook to sell the cargo on shares. Later cargo was carried at fixed rates for merchants, and regular sailings were made at stated intervals. A "packet" service established by the Black Ball Line in 1816 made regular passages from New York to Liverpool, England, in 18 or 20 days. This was the beginning of great steamship lines offering regular sailings on regular routes.

Ships helped knit America together as a united country fronting on two oceans. They brought goods and people from the East coast around the tip of South America to the West coast, and after 1914 by way of the Panama Canal.

American seafaring reached its peak in the clipper-ship days of the 1850's. With the coming of steam, in spite of the *SS Savannah's* triumphant voyage and Robert Fulton's success, America lost the lead among maritime nations, for she lacked the abundant coal close to the sea and the skilled iron workers which Great Britain had. Furthermore, the time and money of explorers and investors were spent building railroads and opening up the West.

Why did our merchant fleet decline after the Civil War?

The Civil War seriously damaged shipping. Many vessels were lost or sold abroad, and after the war, high prices and taxation hampered efforts to revive shipping. England took the lead in building iron and steel hulled vessels powered by steam and using the more efficient screw propeller in place of paddle-wheels.

The American government attempted to help merchant shipping by granting contracts for carrying mail, or by permitting the import of shipbuilding materials without tariffs. Nevertheless, by the beginning of the 20th century, only one American transatlantic line

Left column, from top to bottom:

The transatlantic liner, *Oceanic* (1871), added quite some improvement in comfort for passengers by putting the better cabins on a new deck instead of in separate wooden deckhouses.

Italian liners like this one from 1914, carried thousands of immigrants to the U.S. harbors.

In 1912, shortly before World War I, the first seagoing English diesel-powered vessel, the *Selandia*, entered the cargo service.

The *George Washington*, an ex-German liner, still in her World War I camouflage, carried President Wilson to Europe for the signing of the peace treaty.

was in operation and American ships were carrying less than 10 per cent of United States trade.

In autumn, 1914, the United States found herself a

What part did the merchant marine play in the two World Wars?

neutral country without ships and with a trade crisis. With most of the American ships in the domestic fleet, most exports and imports were being carried on vessels flying foreign flags. When war broke out in Europe, the British Navy virtually locked German merchant ships in port. Allied shipowners, fearing German cruisers, kept their ships in port.

American shipowners started to build ships. When the United States entered the war in 1917, the government inaugurated a very ambitious shipbuilding program. Before that program was finished, more than 2,000 ships had been constructed, but only about 100 of them were completed before the end of the war. About three-quarters of the American expeditionary force was carried overseas to France in allied ships, mostly British. Less than half a million men were carried by a motley fleet composed of American-flag ships engaged in foreign trade, the new war-built ships, and captured German liners.

The tables were turned during World War II, when the allies depended on the United States for assistance with merchant ships. To transport American forces overseas and to supply them and to assist the allies, the United States government launched the biggest shipbuilding program ever undertaken by any nation. In 1944 alone, American shipyards built over 1,880 so-called *Liberty* and *Victory* class ships. This meant that better than 5 cargo-carrying ships a day were placed in our merchant marine service. At the end of the war, the United States had a fleet of over 5,000 merchant ships, over four times the size of the entire American flag fleet at the start of World War II, and equal to three-fifths of the entire world fleet.

In February, 1942, the government took over the direction of ship operation. Ships were taken over from private operators in both domestic and foreign trades; foreign ships were bought; enemy ships in American ports were seized. New methods of loading were devised to use every inch of space and every ton of carrying capacity. Thousands of seamen were recruited and trained to man the ships.

In addition to transporting millions of men and millions of tons of supplies to battlefields in every part of the world, the merchant fleet under control of the War Shipping Administration carried four-fifths of the supplies for the entire war effort. At the same time it brought back essential raw materials for the war effort and supplies needed to maintain the civilian economy. The Army and Navy took many merchant ships as auxiliaries, hospital ships, repair ships, and for other special uses.

When the war was over, merchant ships were busier than ever.

What has happened to the merchant marine in the postwar period?

Half of the seven million troops sent overseas were brought back home within three months after the war's end. Passenger ships converted to troop ships, and every cargo ship that could accommodate even a few men brought the troops home. Hundreds of cargo ships which a few months before had been carrying war supplies were loaded with food, clothing, and machinery to start the rebuilding of European cities shattered in the war.

The U. S. government sought to restore the merchant fleet to private control as quickly as possible. By the end of 1947, all the vessels taken over from private operators had been returned to their owners. Today the total U. S. merchant fleet (active and inactive) of ocean-going vessels numbers about 2,900 ships and new ships are being added all the time.

Merchant ships are indispensable to the economy of a powerful trading nation like the United States with its worldwide commitments. Experience in two world wars and the Korean conflict has demonstrated that the United States must depend on its own merchant fleet and shipbuilding and repair industries for ocean transportation. The maintenance of a strong and efficient merchant marine continues to be essential to trade and defense.

SHIPS FOR DIFFERENT TASKS

Ships are given special designs to suit their tasks. The ships in a modern merchant marine are, first of all, classified as dry-cargo vessels or tankers. The former are designed to carry all types of dry cargo from pins and needles to ores and coal, while the latter are designed to carry

How are merchant ships classified?

cargo that is liquid or semi-fluid. Of the two broad types, the dry-cargo ship is the more complicated. She may be a passenger ship, a freighter, a seatrain, a tramp, or a bulk carrier — or a combination of several of these. (Navy ships have always been in a class by themselves.)

We are inclined to think of the large and luxurious passenger ships as ocean liners and of anything of lesser size or magnificence as a freighter. But a ship — no matter what she carries — is a liner if she (1) is engaged in regular service between fixed ports, (2) follows a regular trade route, and (3) advertises to carry shipments for different shippers to be delivered at various points on the vessel's route. A freighter that fulfills these requirements is frequently called a *cargo liner*.

What are ocean liners?

Hence, a liner may be a passenger ship or a cargo ship, but usually a ship is both. Even the finest and largest passenger ships carry the mails and such high-value "express" freight as fine fabrics and Paris hats, and most modern cargo liners have accommodations for passengers.

A passenger liner derives almost all its income from carrying passengers, and the largest of them are luxurious, seagoing hotels. These fast, graceful vessels are the "queens" of the sea. The longest of these queens is the French *SS France*, 1,035 feet from her flaring stem to the cruiser stern. (Some aircraft carriers, of course,

What are passenger ships?

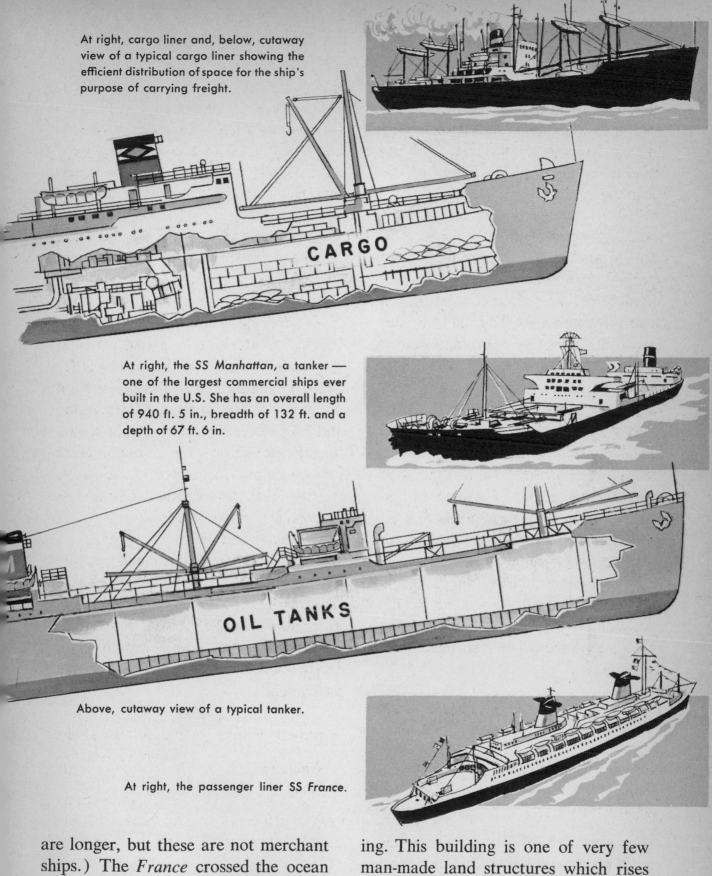

At right, cargo liner and, below, cutaway view of a typical cargo liner showing the efficient distribution of space for the ship's purpose of carrying freight.

CARGO

At right, the SS Manhattan, a tanker — one of the largest commercial ships ever built in the U.S. She has an overall length of 940 ft. 5 in., breadth of 132 ft. and a depth of 67 ft. 6 in.

OIL TANKS

Above, cutaway view of a typical tanker.

At right, the passenger liner SS France.

are longer, but these are not merchant ships.) The *France* crossed the ocean for the first time in 1962. If the *France* were placed on end, she would almost reach the top of the Empire State Build-

ing. This building is one of very few man-made land structures which rises higher than the length of the greatest ships.

The heaviest of the luxury liners is

the *SS Queen Elizabeth*. Tipping the beam at 83,673 tons, this ship is unique in that she may never be surpassed for displacement weight. It would take 40 miles of freight cars to carry the weight of this ship. The *Queen Elizabeth's* rudder alone weighs 140 tons, equal to the entire tonnage of the *Mayflower*, which carred the Pilgrims to the shores of America.

The *SS United States* — the largest passenger ship ever built in America — is the world's fastest ocean liner. On her maiden voyage in 1952, she captured and still holds the Atlantic "Blue Ribbon," the trophy given to the fastest liner, by making the 3,120-mile crossing between Ambrose Lighthouse (United States) and Bishop Rock (England) at an average speed in excess of 35 knots (better than 40 land miles per hour) for an elapsed time of 3 days, 10 hours and 40 minutes. The major dimensions of the *SS United States* are: length, 990 feet, or roughly five city blocks; width,

101 feet, 6 inches; and height from keel to funnel-top, 175 feet, or that of the average 12-story building. She has a total of twelve decks and her galleys can prepare 9,000 meals a day for her 2,000 passengers and 1,000 crewmen. In case she is called into military service, she can transport 14,000 men 10,000 miles without stopping for fuel, water, or supplies. The cost of building the *SS United States* was $70,000,000, or more than one person could spend if he spent a dollar a second for two years.

Not all passenger liners, of course, are as big or fast as these three ships and these three could not enter many of the ports where the smaller ones go. Many of these passenger ships are also in what is called the *cruise service*. That is, they leave one port, stop at many others along the way — permitting their passengers to visit each one — and then return to the original port. The passengers live aboard the ship throughout the entire cruise.

How can a passenger ship be recognized? If you made a trip to one of the major seaports, you would have no trouble picking out the long, sleek passenger liner from other vessels. These liners have hulls topped by two or more *decks,* or stories, of cabins that extend almost the full length of the ship. They also have one or more tall smokestacks or funnels; the forward funnel of the *SS Queen Elizabeth* is 70 feet in height with a cross-section of 44 feet by 30 feet, which would permit three modern locomotives, placed abreast, to pass through. A passenger liner has a great number of portholes in her side — the *SS France* has over 2,000—and a long row of lifeboats is suspended along each side of the ship. Passenger vessels also ride high in the water so that an abundance of air and light is available for the tiers of cabins.

If you were to go aboard a passenger liner, you certainly would have no dif-

ficulty identifying her. Among the passengers' conveniences you would find are swimming pools, theaters, dining rooms, sports deck, observation lounge, ballroom, health baths, gymnasium, shops and a hospital, to say nothing of children's playrooms and kennels for

Cutaway views of the SS *United States* (below) and the *Mayflower* (above), for comparison of size and comfort.

The Cunard liner, Queen Mary, one of the world's largest, has twelve decks.

dogs. Jet airplanes, or no jets, these gracious queens of the sea have proved many times that "getting there is half the fun."

Some ships are designed and constructed to carry fewer passengers and more than just high-value express cargo, and they derive their revenue from both sources. They are somewhat smaller and slower than the larger passenger liners, but offer very fine passenger accommodations. These ships vary greatly in size and in the number of passengers they can handle. Some accommodate more than 800, while others as few as 50. They usually travel to the smaller ports in the Mediterranean, South America, and in the Pacific Ocean.

What are combination ships?

A freighter or cargo liner caters to general cargo, such as automobiles, airplanes and parts, tractors, animals, fresh or frozen fruit, meat or vegetables, and industrial machinery. On certain routes, a cargo liner may carry a hundred or more commodities, for a hundred or more shippers. These workhorses of the sea carry their cargo across the oceans and along the coasts of the world.

What are freighters?

The hull of a freighter is usually shorter than that of a passenger ship, but has the same general appearance. The superstructure of a freighter, however, differs greatly from that of a passenger liner. The cabins of a freighter are generally amidships. Tall masts stand on the deck forward and aft of the cabin section. Long poles called booms are fastened to the bottom of the masts. Cables running from the booms and masts act as cranes to raise and lower cargo through hatchways, or openings in the deck. These hatchways lead to the holds, or storage locations for the cargo. Most freighters carry from 1,000 to 13,000 tons of cargo, depending on their type and the route they travel. Freighters have speeds ranging from 12 to 20 knots and can be identified by the fact that they ride lower in the water, especially when laden, than passenger vessels.

A cargo liner is always built for the particular trade in which its owner is interested. This leads to special features on ships. Those serving tropical ports have refrigerated (called *reefer*) space for frozen and chilled cargo. Such ships carry meat, poultry, and other perishable foodstuffs outbound from the United States, and bring back bananas and other tropical fruits.

Today many freighters carry passengers and some seasoned travelers prefer the informality of this type of ship. Since cargo rather than passengers is the principal source of revenue, accommodations are usually comfortable but simple. Twelve is the maximum number of passengers that can be carried aboard a freighter under international regulations. If more than 12 are carried, the ship is classified as a combination or full passenger ship.

In contrast to the diversified cargoes

What is a tramp freighter?

moved by a cargo liner, a tramp freighter moves one commodity from one port to another port for one shipper and she follows no fixed schedule. Tramps have been called the taxicabs of the sea.

A typical tramp freighter voyage could be something like this: from Liverpool or Cardiff to Argentina with coal, River Plate to Rotterdam or Hamburg with grain, to England in ballast for coal for Argentina again, grain from there to South Africa, ballast to the Philippines for copra for San Francisco, and then to the Pacific Northwest for lumber for Europe. Many European tramp ships sail from home port and are away for several years. Instructions concerning the "next" port and the cargo to be picked up are cabled to the captain.

Tramp ships have been decreasing in importance as a part of the world's merchant fleets. In 1914, nearly half of the world's ships were engaged in the tramping trade. Between World War I and II, this had declined to about 30 per cent of the world's tonnage; and since 1945 the tramp freighter has become still less important.

The dry-cargo bulk carrier is a special

What is a bulk carrier?

ship designed and built to move just one commodity in large amounts or bulk. For example, the col-

Great Lakes bulk carrier.

lier, constructed to carry only coal, has been used for decades.

Bulk carriers resemble freighters, but their employment has a most decided effect on the design of the ship. Their cargoes are usually low-value commodities that must be moved as cheaply as possible, and many of them carry a pay load one way only. Hull design is sacri-

The *President Cleveland*, a combination passenger-cargo ship, is used in the transpacific service.

ficed to maximum cargo capacity and to equipment for mechanical loading and discharging. The typical ore carrier, for instance, is shaped like a long box with flat sides and bottom, except at the bow and stern. Her engines are usually aft and her cabins at the bow and stern. The holds are between these and are made available below by opening the hatches on the long deck. Gravity chutes can fill this space with about 12,000 tons — it would take 240 railroad cars to move the same amount — or more of ore in two hours, and huge cranes can remove the load in eight to ten hours. This is the type of ship used on the Great Lakes to carry iron ore from the Mesabi Range in Minnesota to industrial cities on the lower lakes.

A new type of ship is in the process of being developed to carry **What are seatrains?** general or packaged cargo. These ships are called seatrains, trailer ships, roll-on roll-off, or lift-on lift-off vessels.

There is a reason behind their development. A very large part of the cost of operating a ship occurs in port — loading and discharging cargo. It costs as much to move cargo a few hundred feet from shipside to the hold as it does to move that cargo hundreds of miles at sea. Seatrains are being developed to meet the problem of high costs of cargo handling. With this type of ship, the cargo is placed in some type of container, depending on the type of ship. The container may be a rail car, a trailer truck body, or a standardized container that is either rolled on and off or lifted on and off. A typical "down to the sea in trucks" ship can carry 226 35-foot trailer bodies, 166 below decks and the rest on deck. At shipside, powerful cranes aboard the ship easily lift the trailer bodies for loading. The wheels are left behind, saving space.

The advantages of these ships go beyond the saving on stevedoring costs both at port of loading and port of discharge. Ships receive their revenue for moving cargo over the sea. It is a known fact in the shipping industry that ships earn only when they are at sea, and not when tied up in port. With the new seatrains or trailer ships, shippers now measure the time each ship is in port in terms of hours instead of the days required for traditional cargo handling.

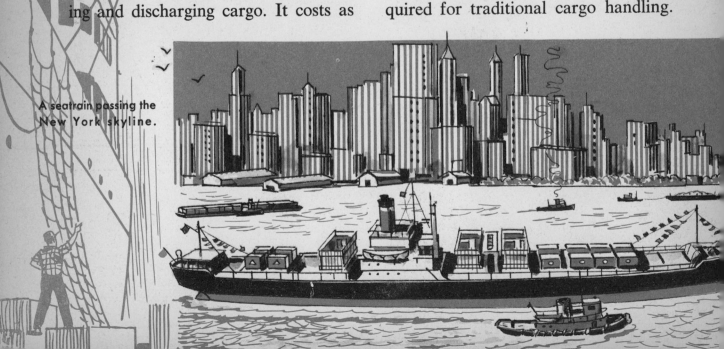

A seatrain passing the New York skyline.

Above, the *Thomas W. Lawson*, the only schooner ever built with seven masts, was constructed in 1902 and used after 1905 by the Sun Oil Company for carrying oil cargoes. At right, the same company's SS *Texas Sun*, a modern supertanker, built in 1960 with a cargo capacity of 373,000 barrels.

There are also benefits to the shipper. Each trailer-container is sealed against burglary, protected against damage, and picked up and delivered without needless delays.

Tankers are vessels built primarily to **What are tankers?** move petroleum or its products. There are, however, some rather interesting variations. For instance, fresh squeezed Florida orange juice is carried to New York City by the tankship *SS Tropicana*. Only 56 hours after her vacuum-sealed, stainless steel tanks are loaded at Cocoa, Florida, the 1,500,000 gallons of orange juice (equivalent to 70 million oranges) are in New York City. Also recently a wine tanker, the *SS Angelo Petri*, was added to the United States merchant marine. She is the world's largest wine tanker, and America's first. The 15,000-ton ship carries over 2.4 million gallons of California wine in 26 vats. The United

States imports much of its molasses in tankers, too.

However, most of the world's tankers are engaged in what this type of ship was developed for — moving petroleum. Today, nearly one ship out of every five sailing the seven seas is a tanker, and since they average larger than dry-cargo ships, they make up one-third of the world's vessel tonnage. A modern tanker can transport 20 or more different types of petroleum and products in its various tanks. Tankers are constructed with an intricate pumping system so that cargo can be loaded or discharged without mixing types.

Tankers resemble cargo ships, except **How can a tanker be recognized?** that cargo space is fitted with tanks and equipment necessary for carrying petroleum or other bulk liquids. The engine room is located in the stern of a tanker in order to keep sparks and heat from the ship's

H

A

R

B

O

R

machinery and boilers from causing an explosion if the vessel carries an inflammable cargo. Some cabin space for the crew is at the stern. The major portion, as well as the tanker's bridge, or control center, is located amidships.

On commercial seagoing vessels, in accordance with maritime tradition, the flag of her country flies from a staff at the extreme stern of the ship. The foremost mast carries the flag of the first country to which the ship is bound. Some vessels fly a private "house" flag, indicating the ship's owner or charterer, from the aftermost mast. The smokestacks are also marked to indicate her shipping owner's line.

How can the nationality of a ship be determined?

If you were to visit a major port in the United States, you would see many harbor ships such as ferries, barges and floats, tugs, fireboats, and a miscellaneous assortment of dredges and other special craft. These harbor ships are workships of the port and perform all the vital tasks necessary for its successful operation. Without them, water commerce and trade could not function.

What is a ferry boat?

In early years, paddle-wheel ferries were used to move back and forth across our harbors. Today most ferries are double-ended vessels, with wheelhouses or control centers, propellers, and rudders at each end to avoid the necessity of turning around at the end of each trip. Their loads include automobiles, trucks and passengers who are mostly commuters living in the suburbs across the harbor and coming to work in the city each day. In recent years, diesel electric-powered ferries have become increasingly common in U. S. harbors.

Although to call a barge a "ship" is a stretch of the imagination, no discussion of shipping and harbor craft would be complete without mentioning them. Harbor barges are of an endless variety, including car-floats, lighter barges, refrigerator barges and tank barges. All of these barges may be built of either wood or steel construction.

What is a barge?

The deck of a car float has two, three, or four railroad tracks installed on it. When she is tied up to her dock, the railroad tracks ashore are joined to the car-float's tracks and freight cars are pushed aboard her and locked in place. These cars can then be either moved across the harbor to another railroad line, or placed alongside a ship and unloaded directly into her hold.

DREDGE

FERRYBOAT

TUGBOAT

The lighter barge is used with package freight — barrels, drums, and other cargoes not in a bulk form. This type of barge has a flat deck and can be tied up to a dock or the side of a ship to transfer her cargo. Many of these barges have shed coverings to protect the cargo against rain and snow damage. There are tank barges employed to transport liquids and chemicals. There are refrigerated barges used to carry frozen foods or chilled meats from cold warehouses to refrigerated freighters.

Barges are also used on inland waterways like rivers, lakes and canals. The so-called "canal barge" is used to carry stone, gravel, sand, and lumber along these waterways and in the harbor.

To protect the harbor against fire, one of its greatest dangers,

What are fireboats and dredges used for?

most major ports have especially equipped vessels to fight ship, dock and shoreside fires.

Fireboats also traditionally greet ships on their maiden or first voyages with sprays of water.

Many ports also have harbor police boats to patrol the harbor for thieves and piracy.

Most harbors must keep dredges busy throughout the year to prevent the silt, mud and sand carried down river by the current or in from the ocean from choking the harbor. Dredge sizes range all the way from the small harbor type to large offshore craft. Such craft are long or short, squat or high, stationary or self-propelled, yet they are usually one of two types — suction or dipper. On the former, large hoses are placed on the bottom and powerful suction pumps on the dredge itself suck up the mud and sand. This is washed through long pipes, mounted on floats, to shore where it fills in holes or changes the shore line.

The dipper type dredges have a large bucket similar to those we see on steamshovels and actually looks like a steam-

FIREBOAT

BARGE

shovel floating on water. The bucket plunges open-mouthed into the mud and then closes to pick up a bucket load of silt. This is dropped on a barge. When the barge is filled, she is towed into harbor and the silt is used for filling in swamps and lowlands.

Tugs are very numerous in any harbor,

What is the purpose of tugboats?

but there are many types used for different tasks. For instance, there are float tugs, which move car floats; transfer tugs, which move barges; and drill tugs, which move both barges and floats on short hauls. There are tugs solely concerned with the docking of big ships. Others, while seemingly identical in size with harbor tugs, are actually larger physically; their propulsion machinery is far more powerful and they are engaged in towing several canal barges. There are also seagoing tugs. While harbor tugs are rarely more than 110 feet, these ocean-going vessels are usually considerably larger. Most modern tugs are constructed of steel and have either diesel or diesel-electric engines.

On inland waterways, the predominant craft are towboats, or push boats. These are a very powerful type of harbor tug that tows a load of barges. On these waterways "towing" is really "pushing." With the tow pushing, it is easier to steer and water resistance is lowered by having the barges ahead out of the wake of the ship's propellers. Some of the modern inland towboats connected to their barges engaged in the petroleum trade on the Mississippi and Ohio Rivers would dwarf the *SS Queen Elizabeth* or even the *SS France*, the longest luxury passenger liner, in total overall length. The length of many tank barges plus the towboat is over 1150 feet, as compared to the *SS France's* 1035 feet. These powerful diesel-powered vessels are supplanting the picturesque wooden, steam-driven, stern paddle-wheel towboats on the major river waterways.

There are also many other special-pur-

What are "whaling factories?"

pose ships afloat. Being designed for some particular job, they often are not

The *Queen Elizabeth,* with an overall length of 1031 feet, is dwarfed by this modern integrated petroleum tow of the Ohio river. The length of the towboat with tank barges is 1170 feet.

TANK BARGES

TOWBOAT

QUEEN ELIZABETH

The whale is harpooned with a cannon on board of the modern "killerboat," one of the auxiliary vessels of the "whaling factory."

The dead whale is inflated with compressed air and marked with a flag.

Once aboard, the whale is dismembered and soon only the giant jawbone is left to be thrown overboard.
The modern whaling "factory-ship" with a whale being towed aboard through the giant opening in the stern of the craft.

built by the conventional designs. All warships are special-purpose vessels, and although they have played such a great and important part in the world's history, they have not contributed nearly so much to the art of naval architecture as have the merchant ships.

Perhaps the biggest special-purpose merchant vessels are the "whaling factories." These huge ships, which in outward appearance are similar to a large freighter, do not do the actual hunting of the whales, but employ a fleet of smaller vessels to do the harpooning and the killing. Once a whale is dead, it is inflated with compressed air and towed back to the factory ship, where it is hauled on deck through a square slipway in the stern. The whale is then cut up, the blubber rendered into oil, and the meat refrigerated. Little is wasted. These floating factories, some of which

LARGE TRAWLER

MOTOR TRAWLER

are over 650 feet long, are equipped with the most modern of scientific apparatus and can even produce medical and vitamin preparations on board.

There are all types of fishing vessels afloat on waters of the world. The design of the ship depends on several factors, such as variation of catch, closeness to markets, how far the fishermen must go to make their catches, and original cost of the vessel. Many sailing vessels — some even resembling those of the 17th century — are still used. In the United States, the schooner (see page 15) and diesel-motor trawlers are used by most of our commercial fishermen. The trawler looks much like an ocean-going tug, except that many of earlier designs had a turtle-backed forecastle, which was believed to permit the pounding seas to flow over the side faster. Most of our modern trawlers have abandoned this feature. Some of the larger fishing trawlers are over 200 feet and are actually floating canning factories with facilities to can the fish after they are caught. Trawlers must be constructed to move about the waters in the worst kinds of weather. The trawler usually tows her bag-shaped fish nets over the sea bed in hopes of making good catches for her owners.

SARDINE BOAT

EUROPEAN TUNA FISHING BOAT

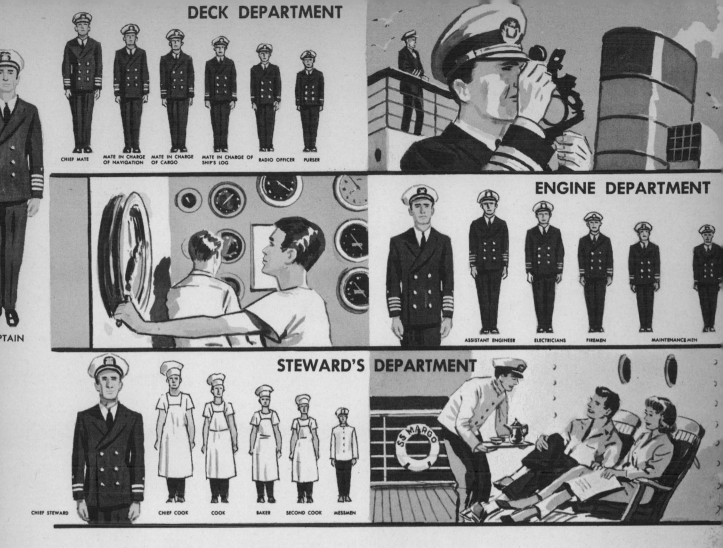

DECK DEPARTMENT

CHIEF MATE · MATE IN CHARGE OF NAVIGATION · MATE IN CHARGE OF CARGO · MATE IN CHARGE OF SHIP'S LOG · RADIO OFFICER · PURSER

CAPTAIN

ENGINE DEPARTMENT

ASSISTANT ENGINEER · ELECTRICIANS · FIREMEN · MAINTENANCE MEN

STEWARD'S DEPARTMENT

CHIEF STEWARD · CHIEF COOK · COOK · BAKER · SECOND COOK · MESSMEN

Sailors of Today

Who mans a merchant ship? When a ship puts to sea, she carries a highly organized crew commanded by *licensed officers*. The officers include the captain, or master, and his assistants (called either mates or officers), the chief engineer, and the assistant engineers. Under the officers come the crewmen who are given names in accordance with the job they do aboard ship.

The captain, or master, is responsible for the condition and safety of the ship, crew, passengers and cargo. He is legal representative of the ship's owners. He is chief navigator, although he may assign the duties of that position to some subordinate, usually the second officer.

He is responsible for discipline, acting as both judge and jury as circumstances demand. On passenger ships he is host to the ship's guests. The ship is "worked" at all times under his general or special orders. The crew of his ship is divided into three departments — deck, engine, and steward's.

A ship's crew is divided into groups called watches. All American ships except the smallest types are required by the Merchant Marine Act of 1936 to carry officers and men enough for three watches. Each watch serves or stands two work turns of four hours each. In emergencies or for heavy tasks, the order *"All hands"* will summon the entire crew.

The first ship of the Navy's surface nuclear fleet was the aircraft carrier *Enterprise* (left), launched in 1960. She is about five city blocks long (1,100 ft.), and measures 252 ft. at her widest point.

The battleship *Missouri* (below left) was, just like the *Wisconsin,* one of the last floating fortresses used by the U.S. Navy.

To protect carriers, the first of many atomic powered cruisers, the *Long Beach* (below right), was launched in 1961 dnd carries long-range Polaris missiles instead of conventional cruiser guns.

Ships that Protect Our Nation

What is the function of the U. S. Navy? The use and control of the sea is and has been a most important factor in the history of the world. Control of the seas in wartime is the function of the U. S. Navy. In time of war, the Navy must gain and keep this control against enemy attacks from the air, on the sea, and under the sea. It must guard friendly merchant shipping. The Navy also must transport troops, equipment, and supplies to foreign shores for counter-attacks; in addition, its guns and planes give support to these attacks.

In time of peace, Navy ships speed on

A convoy of World War II Liberty ships and troop carriers, protected by destroyers.

U.S. NAVY HOSPITAL SHIP *REPOSE*

MINESWEEPER

57

TORPEDO BOAT

The Navy played a very important part in the invasion of the Normandy beaches in 1944.

errands of mercy, such as carrying food and medical supplies to disaster-stricken areas. They also take part in many rescue operations at sea. The tasks and functions of the U. S. Navy, in either war or peace, seldom vary, although the ships, weapons and tactics needed to accomplish them constantly change.

What types of ships make up a modern navy? The modern navy is made up of many different types of ships, each of which is constructed to fulfill a specific task or duty. Because of the air age, the aircraft carrier has been the chief warship on the sea. Other members of the fighting team include the cruisers, destroyers, and submarines. (Until recently, the battleship was a member of this team, too.) To service these warships, the Navy employs about 50 types of auxiliary ships such as tankers, ocean tugs, repair ships, mine layers, mine sweepers, patrol craft, submarine chasers, oilers, hospital ships, amphibious landing craft, and so on.

It is a far cry from the first American submarine, the *Turtle*, to the first American atomic submarine, the *Nautilus*. The *Turtle*, which looked like two turtle shells joined together, was built by David Bushnell in 1776. The *Nautilus* was launched in 1954.

TURTLE

The Lifeguards and Policemen of the Sea

What is the purpose of the U. S. Coast Guard? The founder of the U. S. Coast Guard was Alexander Hamilton, first Secretary of the Treasury. In 1790, he asked Congress to provide a fleet of 10 armed cutters to insure the collection of tonnage dues and import duties from vessels entering United States waters. Today, the U. S. Coast Guard is one of the more important and far-flung services under the Stars and Stripes. Wherever the going is rough, there is the Coast Guard . . . far at sea, on the surface and in the air, on ice and weather patrol (an international service), along the wind-swept beaches of all U. S. shores, and wherever shipping runs the danger of reefs, shoals or rocks. In other words, the members of the Coast Guard are the lifeguards and policemen of the sea.

Harbor patrol boat on police duty and Coast Guard lightship, the latter, right, especially equipped with beacons, fog signals and lights.

Below, the Coast Guard icebreaker, *Eastwind,* leads a cargo ship through ice flow.

Below right, Coast Guard cutter on its way to service a lighthouse.

How Ships Are Built

How is a ship designed?

The maritime industries consist of two main branches: shipbuilding and the shipping industry, or ship operation. During the early years of American history, these two industries were closely associated. The builder of the ship constructed it for his own use, and owned and operated the ship.

As the ship became more complicated and larger, her construction called for the special skills and facilities found only in the yards of large shipbuilding companies. Modern vessels are constructed by these companies for one particular steamship company or line. Needless to say, a steamship company orders a vessel designed to suit the particular trade in which it engages. The information given the builder by the company includes the route the vessel will travel, the cargo she will carry, her size and speed desired, the type of machinery the ship should have, and how much space will be needed for cargo, passengers, or both.

Marine or naval architects and engineers then design the ship to meet the company's specifications. An important consideration in any design is that the ship will be both economical to construct and profitable to operate. The ship's design must also comply with the strict government safety regulations. In administering the Merchant Marine Safety Program, the Coast Guard is associated with nearly every phase of the life of an American ship from the first plans on the drafting board to the final trip to the scrap yard. Among the duties which the Coast Guard must carry out are the periodic inspection of hulls, machinery and equipment of merchant vessels to insure seaworthiness and compliance with safety regulations, the approval of plans prior to construction or conversion, and an extensive first inspection of all new vessels.

Construction on a new ship begins in the *mold loft,* a very large room where draftsmen make paper patterns, called *templates,* for each piece of steel that will be used in the vessel's building. On each template every cut, band, flange, angle, or roll is accurately indicated. The ship fitter then transfers these marks to the steel plates, much in the same manner a dressmaker does her dress patterns on cloth. The marked steel plates are then cut, punched, bent, or rolled into

How is the construction work accomplished on a ship?

the desired shapes. When this is completed, the steel pieces move to the subassembly shops to be joined together to make large parts, or go directly to the construction site to be placed into their proper position.

The actual assembling of the ship begins with the laying of the *keel* or the backbone of the vessel. First, however, the *building ways* or slip for the vessel is prepared at the water's edge. Keel blocks — short heavy timbers with the upper surface shaped to the keel line — are set up with a slight incline toward the water. On these blocks is laid the keel, generally composed of a number of thick plates or bars of steel riveted or welded to make the desired thickness and length.

Once the keel is laid, the middle sections are constructed by adding steel beams or ribs. These ribs, of course, support and shape the hull. While the

PATTERN ON STEEL

middle sections are being built, the ship's necessary machinery and boilers are installed in place. Next the metal plates are electrically welded to the framework to produce the hull itself.

Before long, the graceful shape of the hull can be seen. Most ships are built with double bottoms, which lessen damage to vessels in case of an accident. The space between the bottoms, in which an average man can almost stand upright at the center of the hull, is used for storing oil for the engines or fresh water for the boilers. As the building proceeds, the bulkheads, or crosswise and lengthwise partitions, which divide the ship into her many watertight compartments, are constructed and welded into place. Actually, the more numerous these watertight compartments, the less the danger of sinking. The doors of the compartments must also be watertight and are provided with closing apparatus

Above left, ships in various stages of completion in an American shipyard, and, above, an exciting moment: the huge propeller is being mounted.

electrically controlled from several central locations, so that any or all can be closed in a second by pushing a button. Most large ships built today have a "collision bulkhead" in the bow. It is built to be especially strong to withstand ramming and to confine any damage to that section of the ship should the bow become pushed in. To complete the boat for launching, the steel decks and the superstructure are welded in place on their beams or ribs.

The hull is usually launched as soon

How is a ship launched? as it will float; the outfitting of the ship is completed in the water. Most ships are launched stern first. Sometimes, however, sidewise launchings are necessary when the shipyard is built on a plot of land too narrow to permit lengthwise building ways or when the width of the waterway in front of the shipyard is restricted.

To get the hull ready for launching, workmen lay *groundways* or *slipways* along each side of the keel blocks the full extent of the vessel and into the water. The groundways are long, greased wood timbers and it is on these that the ship will slide into the water. To support the vessel's weight on groundways after the keel blocks are removed, a launching cradle is built.

The ship rides on this cradle into the water until she floats. The launching must be as carefully planned as the building, because some ships have been wrecked by mistakes at this time.

The actual christening or launching ceremony is a picturesque occasion. A woman designated by the builder as the ship's sponsor breaks a bottle of champagne — a symbol of the blood sacrifice which marked a launching in pagan days — over the bow as she names the ship. The vessel is released down the groundways just as the bottle breaks and slides into the water due to her own weight.

Some giant pasenger liners, aircraft carriers, and huge tankers are built in *graving basins*, or graving docks as they are also called, which are somewhat like huge bathtubs sunk below the level of the bathroom floor. At the outboard end (closest to the water) however, there is a gate. To launch a ship from this type of dock, the gate is opened and water rushes into the basin until it is filled. The ship can then be towed away from the work area. To remove the water from the graving dock, the gate is closed and the basin is pumped dry.

After the ship is launched, tugs pull her

When is a ship released to her owner? to an outfitting dock where all the construction work is completed. Her interior fittings and decorations are added, and all the machinery and engines are tuned up for the builder's trials or tests.

During these sea trials, every piece of machinery is tested; every cable is

All's well that ends well! In ship building it is the successful launch.

proved and the instruments calibrated. The anchor gear is tried and the ship is swung slowly in a circle while her compasses are adjusted. Then comes a steaming trial in which the engineers check all gauges and fuel consumption is determined. The final test is the speed trial.

If the ship returns from her trial runs with a large broom tied to the mast, she has made a "clean sweep" of her tests. All that remains is hauling down the builder's flag from the aftermost mast and hoisting the owner's house-flag in its place. The ship is then formally turned over to her owners.

Ships of the Future

Since we are now living in the age of the atom, it seems clear that a greater use of nuclear ships is just a matter of time. Nuclear-powered ships of the future will certainly make our present efforts seem as old-fashioned as the *NS-Savannah's* namesake, the *SS Savannah*, appears to us today.

While all atomic-powered ships built in the near future will be driven by steam turbines, eventually, the more efficient gas turbines will probably replace them. A gas turbine could be said to be a form of jet-propulsion. In this system, however, the hot gas jet, instead of acting directly in air as in a reaction engine — like the rocket or airplane — is used to drive a normal turbo-electric drive and screw propeller. The gas system has the big advantage of occupying small space in a ship compared with a steam turbine and boilers. Engineers are designing gas turbines for ships.

The hulls of our ships of the future will also change. While *hydrofoils* were used on small craft for some time, only recently small passenger liners have been employing them. The hydrofoil is a fin on an arm, shaped like an airplane wing to give it lifting power, that extends from the side of a ship. When the vessel travels fast enough, a set of these hydrofoils lifts the ship so that the hull is in the air and only the hydrofoils and the propeller are submerged. The ship's speed can be increased by their use because the hull is not being pushed through the water. The ride is smoother, too, since the ship is lifted above the water. A recent improvement is the electronic control of the lift so that the hydrofoils are automatically adjusted to the height of the waves.

Research is also going on with so-called *surface-effect* ships. This type of vessel will travel at a very low height above the water, supported by a cushion of air trapped below the bottom of the ship. Such vessels will be very fast and will give a smooth ride.

While research is going on to make our waterways more like roadways, some marine designers are at work on nuclear-powered underwater or submarine cargo ships. In the design of such vessels, the cargo hull with its holds will

While nuclear powered submarines have been in service since the launching of the *Nautilus* in 1954, and nuclear powered Navy surface ships since the launching of the *Enterprise* in 1960, the first nuclear powered merchant ship, the *Savannah*, above, was not completed until 1962.

The surface-effect principle, by which downward thrusting jets of air cause the ship to rise above the surface of water and thus ride on a cushion of air, enable it to travel at very high speeds.

The first oceangoing hydrofoil ship, the *H.S. Denison*, was launched in 1962.

be beneath the water and the living quarters of the crew are above water in a special gondola.

Work is going on all the time to improve living quarters aboard ship, to make methods of cargo handling better, to find more efficient operating procedures, and to find new navigating techniques. Thus, the scientific achievements of our age will be employed to keep the American ships in the forefront of progress.

Acknowledgements: The author would like to thank the following for their technical help and for use of their photographs: The Propeller Club of the United States; U. S. Department of Commerce, Maritime Administration; U. S. Navy; U. S. Coast Guard; Moran Towing & Transportation Company; Port of New York Authority; United States Lines; French Line; and Cunard Line.